FAVORITE BRAND NAME

Easy Home Cooking

SHORTCUT
SUPPERS

Publications International, Ltd.
Favorite Brand Name Recipes at www.fbnr.com

Pictured on the front cover: Chicken Paprikash *(page 20).*

Pictured on the back cover *(left to right):* Strawberry Margarita Pie *(page 60)* and Teriyaki Beef *(page 21).*

ISBN: 0-7853-4357-1

Manufactured in China.

8 7 6 5 4 3 2 1

Microwave Cooking: Microwave ovens vary in wattage. Use the cooking times as guidelines and check for doneness before adding more time.

CONTENTS

p. 30

ALL YOU NEED IS FOUR

Seafood Risotto

▮▮▮

1 package (5.2 ounces) rice in creamy sauce (Risotto Milanese flavor)
1 package (14 to 16 ounces) frozen fully cooked shrimp
1 box (10 ounces) BIRDS EYE® frozen Mixed Vegetables
2 teaspoons grated Parmesan cheese

• In 4-quart saucepan, prepare rice according to package directions. Add frozen shrimp and vegetables during last 10 minutes.

• Sprinkle with cheese.
Makes 4 servings

Serving Suggestion: Serve with garlic bread and a tossed green salad.

Prep Time: 5 minutes
Cook Time: 15 minutes

Hot & Spicy Buffalo Chicken Wings

▐▐▐

1 can (15 ounces) DEL MONTE® Original Sloppy Joe Sauce
¼ cup thick and chunky salsa, medium
1 tablespoon red wine vinegar or cider vinegar
20 chicken wings (about 4 pounds)

1. Preheat oven to 400°F.

2. Combine sloppy joe sauce, salsa and vinegar in small bowl. Remove ¼ cup sauce mixture to serve with cooked chicken wings; cover and refrigerate. Set aside remaining sauce mixture.

3. Arrange wings in single layer in large, shallow baking pan; brush wings with sauce mixture.

4. Bake chicken, uncovered, on middle rack in oven 35 minutes or until chicken is no longer pink in center, turning and brushing with remaining sauce mixture after 15 minutes. Serve with reserved ¼ cup sauce. Garnish, if desired.

Makes 4 servings

Prep Time: 5 minutes
Cook Time: 35 minutes

Lite Teriyaki Pork Chops

▐▐▐

½ cup KIKKOMAN® Lite Teriyaki Marinade & Sauce
2 tablespoons prepared horseradish
⅛ teaspoon ground cinnamon
4 pork rib or loin chops, ¾ inch thick

Blend lite teriyaki sauce, horseradish and cinnamon; pour over chops in large plastic food storage bag. Press air out of bag; close top securely. Turn bag over several times to coat all chops well. Refrigerate 1½ hours, turning bag over occasionally. Reserving marinade, remove chops. Place chops on grill 5 to 7 inches from medium-hot coals. Cook 10 to 12 minutes, or until light pink in center, turning over and brushing occasionally with reserved marinade. (Or, place chops on rack of broiler pan. Broil 5 to 7 inches from heat 8 to 10 minutes, or until light pink in center, turning over and brushing occasionally with reserved marinade.)

Makes 4 servings

Hot & Spicy Buffalo Chicken Wings

Country Herb Roasted Chicken

∎∎∎

1 chicken (2½ to 3 pounds), cut into serving pieces (with or without skin) *or* 1½ pounds boneless skinless chicken breast halves
1 envelope LIPTON® Recipe Secrets® Savory Herb with Garlic Soup Mix
2 tablespoons water
1 tablespoon olive or vegetable oil

Preheat oven to 375°F.

In 13×9-inch baking or roasting pan, arrange chicken. In small bowl, combine remaining ingredients; brush on chicken.

For chicken pieces, bake uncovered 45 minutes or until chicken is no longer pink. For chicken breast halves, bake uncovered 20 minutes or until chicken is no longer pink.
Makes about 4 servings

Menu Suggestion: Serve with a lettuce and tomato salad, scalloped potatoes and cooked green beans.

Country Herb Roasted Chicken

Ravioli with Roasted Red Pepper Alfredo Sauce

▌▌▌

1 package (10 ounces) DiGIORNO® Roasted Red Bell Pepper Cream Sauce
½ cup toasted chopped walnuts
1 package (9 ounces) DiGIORNO® Four Cheese Ravioli, cooked, drained

HEAT sauce and walnuts in saucepan on medium heat.

TOSS with hot ravioli. Sprinkle with additional toasted chopped walnuts and chopped fresh parsley, if desired.

Makes 4 servings

Prep Time: 10 minutes
Cook Time: 10 minutes

Grilled Fresh Fish

▌▌▌

3 to 3½ pounds fresh tuna or catfish
¾ cup prepared HIDDEN VALLEY® Original Ranch® Salad Dressing
Chopped fresh dill
Lemon wedges (optional)

Place fish on heavy-duty foil. Cover with salad dressing. Grill over medium-hot coals until fish turns opaque and flakes easily when tested with fork, 20 to 30 minutes. Or broil fish 15 to 20 minutes. Sprinkle with dill; garnish with lemon wedges, if desired.

Makes 6 servings

Easy Veg-All® Potato Casserole

▌▌▌

1 (5.5-ounce) package au gratin potatoes
1 (15-ounce) can VEG-ALL® Mixed Vegetables, drained
1 cup cooked, cubed ham, turkey or chicken
2 tablespoons bread crumbs

Combine au gratin potatoes, vegetables and ham in medium casserole. Sprinkle with bread crumbs. Cook according to au gratin potatoes package directions. Cool 5 minutes before serving.

Makes 6 servings

Peachy Pork Roast

▌▌▌

1 (3 to 4-pound) rolled
    boneless pork loin roast
1 cup (12-ounce jar)
    SMUCKER'S® Currant
    Jelly
½ cup SMUCKER'S® Peach
    Preserves
    Fresh peach slices and
    currants for garnish, if
    desired

Insert meat thermometer into one end of roast. Bake at 325°F for 30 to 40 minutes or until browned. Turn roast and bake an additional 30 minutes to brown the bottom. Turn roast again and drain off drippings.

In saucepan over medium heat, melt currant jelly and peach preserves. Brush roast generously with sauce.

Continue baking until meat thermometer reads 160°F, about 15 minutes, basting occasionally with sauce.

Remove roast from oven. Garnish with peach slices and currants. Serve with remaining sauce.

Makes 8 to 10 servings

Note: Canned, sliced peaches can be substituted for fresh peaches.

Holiday Vegetable Bake

▌▌▌

1 package (16 ounces) frozen
    vegetable combination
1 can (10¾ ounces)
    condensed cream of
    broccoli soup
⅓ cup milk
1⅓ cups FRENCH'S® French
    Fried Onions, divided

Microwave Directions:
Combine vegetables, soup, milk and ⅔ *cup* French Fried Onions in 2-quart microwavable casserole. Microwave,* uncovered, on HIGH 10 to 12 minutes or until vegetables are crisp-tender, stirring halfway through cooking time. Sprinkle with remaining ⅔ *cup* onions. Microwave 1 minute or until onions are golden.

Makes 4 to 6 servings

Prep Time: 5 minutes
Cook Time: 10 minutes

*Or, bake in preheated 375°F oven 30 to 35 minutes.

Swiss Rosti Potatoes

▐▐▐

4 large Russet potatoes (about 6 ounces each)*
4 tablespoons butter or margarine
Salt and pepper

* Prepare potatoes several hours or up to 1 day in advance.

1. Preheat oven to 400°F. To prepare potatoes, pierce each potato in several places with fork. Bake 1 hour or until fork-tender. Cool completely, then refrigerate.

2. When potatoes are cold, peel with paring knife. Grate potatoes by hand with large section of metal grater or use food processor with large grater disk.

3. Heat butter in 10-inch skillet over medium-high heat until melted and bubbly. Press grated potatoes evenly into skillet. (Do not stir or turn potatoes.) Season with salt and pepper to taste. Cook 10 to 12 minutes until golden brown.

4. Turn off heat; invert serving plate over skillet. Turn potatoes out onto plate. Garnish, if desired. Serve immediately.

Makes 4 side-dish servings

Grilled Sausage with Apricot-Mustard Glaze

▐▐▐

½ cup SMUCKER'S® Apricot Preserves
½ cup Dijon mustard
1 pound smoked pork sausage
4 French sandwich rolls

Combine preserves and mustard; blend well. Set aside.

Cut pork sausage into 2-inch pieces and place on baking sheet. Grill or broil 4 minutes; turn and cook another 4 minutes.

Remove baking sheet from heat and dip each piece in apricot-mustard glaze. Return to broiler or grill and cook 2 more minutes or until lightly browned. Divide among sandwich rolls; serve with additional apricot-mustard glaze on the side.

Makes 4 servings

Swiss Rosti Potatoes

SNAPPY

Skillet Suppers

Chicken Étouffé with Pasta

▌▌▌

¼ cup vegetable oil
⅓ cup all-purpose flour
½ cup finely chopped onion
4 boneless skinless chicken breast halves (about 1¼ pounds), cut into ¼-inch-thick strips
1 cup chicken broth
1 medium tomato, chopped
¾ cup sliced celery
1 medium green bell pepper, chopped
2 teaspoons Creole or Cajun seasoning blend
Hot cooked pasta

1. Heat oil in large skillet over medium heat until hot. Add flour; cook and stir 10 minutes or until dark brown. Add onion. Cook and stir 2 minutes.

2. Stir in chicken, broth, tomato, celery, bell pepper and seasoning blend. Cook 8 minutes or until chicken is no longer pink in center. Serve over pasta.

Makes 6 servings

Prep and Cook Time:
25 minutes

Walnut Chicken

▐▐▐

3 tablespoons soy sauce
2 tablespoons minced fresh
   ginger
1 tablespoon cornstarch
1 tablespoon rice wine
2 cloves garlic, minced
¼ to ½ teaspoon red pepper
   flakes
1 pound boneless skinless
   chicken thighs, diced
3 tablespoons vegetable oil
½ cup walnut halves or pieces
1 cup frozen cut green beans,
   thawed
½ cup sliced water chestnuts
2 green onions with tops, cut
   into 1-inch pieces
¼ cup water
   Hot cooked rice

Combine soy sauce, ginger, cornstarch, wine, garlic and red pepper in large bowl; stir until smooth. Add chicken; toss. Marinate 10 minutes.

Heat wok or large skillet over high heat about 1 minute or until hot. Drizzle oil into wok and heat 30 seconds. Add walnuts; stir-fry about 1 minute or until lightly browned. Remove to small bowl. Add chicken mixture to wok; stir-fry about 5 to 7 minutes or until chicken is no longer pink in center. Add beans, water chestnuts, onions and water; stir-fry until heated through. Serve over rice. Sprinkle with walnuts.   *Makes 4 servings*

Walnut Chicken

Meatball Stroganoff with Rice

▮ ▮ ▮

MEATBALLS
1 egg, lightly beaten
1½ pounds ground beef round
⅓ cup plain dry bread crumbs
1 tablespoon Worcestershire sauce
1 teaspoon salt
¼ teaspoon pepper
2 tablespoons CRISCO® Vegetable Oil

SAUCE
1 tablespoon CRISCO® Vegetable Oil
½ pound mushrooms, sliced
2 tablespoons all-purpose flour
1 teaspoon ketchup
1 can (10½ ounces) condensed, double strength beef broth (bouillon), undiluted*
½ (1-ounce) envelope dry onion soup mix (about 2 tablespoons)
1 cup sour cream

4 cups hot cooked rice

* 1¼ cups reconstituted beef broth made with double amount of very low sodium beef broth granules may be substituted for beef broth (bouillon).

1. For meatballs, combine egg, meat, bread crumbs, Worcestershire sauce, salt and pepper in large bowl. Mix until well blended. Shape into eighteen 2-inch meatballs.

2. Heat 2 tablespoons Crisco® Oil in large skillet on medium heat. Add meatballs. Brown on all sides. Reduce heat to low. Cook 10 minutes. Remove meatballs from skillet.

3. For sauce, add 1 tablespoon Crisco® Oil to skillet. Add mushrooms. Cook and stir 4 minutes. Remove skillet from heat.

4. Stir in flour and ketchup until blended. Stir in broth gradually. Add soup mix. Return to heat. Bring to a boil on medium heat. Reduce heat to low. Simmer 2 minutes. Return meatballs to skillet. Heat thoroughly, stirring occasionally.

5. Stir in sour cream. Heat but do not bring to a boil. Serve over hot rice. Garnish, if desired.   *Makes 6 servings*

Bratwurst Skillet

■ ■ ■

1 pound bratwurst links, cut into ½-inch slices
1½ cups green bell pepper strips
1½ cups red bell pepper strips
1½ cups sliced onions
1 teaspoon paprika
1 teaspoon caraway seeds

1. Heat large skillet over medium heat until hot. Add bratwurst; cover and cook about 5 minutes or until browned and no longer pink in center. Transfer bratwurst to plate. Cover and keep warm.

2. Drain all but 1 tablespoon drippings from skillet. Add bell peppers, onions, paprika and caraway seeds. Cook and stir about 5 minutes or until vegetables are tender.

3. Combine bratwurst and vegetables. Serve immediately.

Makes 4 servings

Cutting Corners: To make this even speedier, purchase a packaged stir-fry pepper and onion mix and use in place of the bell peppers and onions.

Prep and Cook Time: 18 minutes

Frittata Primavera

■ ■ ■

1 medium onion, chopped
1 medium red or green bell pepper, cut into strips
1 medium potato, peeled and grated (about 1 cup)
1 cup coarsely chopped broccoli
1 teaspoon dried oregano leaves, crushed
⅛ teaspoon ground black pepper
1 tablespoon FLEISCHMANN'S® Original Spread (70% Corn Oil)
1 (8-ounce) container EGG BEATERS® Healthy Real Egg Substitute

In 10-inch nonstick skillet or omelet pan, cook and stir onion, bell pepper, potato, broccoli, oregano and black pepper in spread until vegetables are tender-crisp.

In small bowl, with electric mixer at high speed, beat Egg Beaters® for 2 minutes until light and fluffy; pour over vegetables. Cover and cook over medium heat for 5 to 7 minutes until eggs are set. Serve from pan or carefully invert onto warm serving plate. Serve immediately.

Makes 4 servings

Bratwurst Skillet

Chicken Paprikash

▌▌▌

3 tablespoons butter
3½ cups thinly sliced onions
2 cups red bell pepper strips
4 large cloves garlic, minced
2½ tablespoons all-purpose
    flour
4 teaspoons paprika
2 cups chicken broth
2 tablespoons tomato paste
1½ pounds boneless skinless
    chicken breasts, trimmed
    and cut into 1-inch strips
Salt and pepper to taste
1 cup sour cream
1 pound cooked extra-wide
    egg noodles
1 tablespoon minced parsley

Melt butter in large skillet over medium heat. Add onions, bell peppers and garlic; stir well. Cover and cook 15 minutes, stirring occasionally. Do not let vegetables brown; reduce heat if necessary. Stir in flour and paprika. Cook and stir 1 to 2 minutes, until completely blended. Add chicken broth and tomato paste; stir. Increase heat to medium. Cook and stir until sauce comes to a boil. Add chicken. Stir until mixture returns to a boil. Reduce heat to low. Cover and cook 15 to 20 minutes or until chicken is no longer pink in center, stirring occasionally. Season with salt and pepper to taste.

Place sour cream in small bowl. Slowly pour ¼ cup thickened sauce into sour cream, stirring constantly until blended. Repeat with additional ¼ cup. Slowly pour sour cream mixture back into skillet, stirring constantly to prevent sour cream from separating. Serve immediately over hot noodles. Sprinkle with parsley.

Makes 6 servings

Beef with Cabbage and Carrots

▌▌▌

¾ pound extra-lean (90% lean)
    ground beef
4 cups shredded cabbage
1½ cups shredded carrot
    (1 large carrot)
½ teaspoon caraway seeds
2 tablespoons seasoned rice
    vinegar
Salt and freshly ground
    pepper

Brown ground beef in large skillet. Drain. Reduce heat to low. Stir in cabbage, carrot and caraway seeds; cover. Cook 10 minutes or until vegetables are tender, stirring occasionally. Stir in vinegar. (Add 1 tablespoon water for extra moistness, if desired.) Season with salt and pepper to taste.

Makes 4 servings

Teriyaki Beef

███

¾ pound sirloin tip steak, cut
    into thin strips
½ cup teriyaki sauce
¼ cup water
1 tablespoon cornstarch
1 teaspoon sugar
1 bag (16 ounces) BIRDS
    EYE® frozen Farm Fresh
    Mixtures Broccoli,
    Carrots and Water
    Chestnuts

• Spray large skillet with
nonstick cooking spray; cook
beef strips over medium-high
heat 7 to 8 minutes, stirring
occasionally.

• Combine teriyaki sauce,
water, cornstarch and sugar;
mix well.

• Add teriyaki sauce mixture
and vegetables to beef. Bring to
boil; quickly reduce heat to
medium.

• Cook 7 to 10 minutes or until
broccoli is heated through,
stirring occasionally.

Makes 4 to 6 servings

Prep Time: 5 to 10 minutes
Cook Time: 20 minutes

Cajun Pork Skillet Dinner

███

1 tablespoon vegetable oil
4 rib-cut pork chops* (about
    1 pound), cut ¾ inch
    thick
1 jar (16 ounces) chunky
    medium salsa
1⅓ cups FRENCH'S® French
    Fried Onions, divided
½ teaspoon dried thyme
    leaves
    Cooked white rice
    (optional)

** Or, substitute 1 pound boneless skinless
chicken breasts for pork chops.*

Heat oil in large nonstick skillet.
Add pork chops; cook about 5
minutes or until browned on
both sides.

Stir in salsa, *⅔ cup* French Fried
Onions and thyme. Bring to a
boil over high heat. Reduce
heat to medium-low. Cover;
cook 10 minutes or until pork
is no longer pink near bone,
stirring occasionally. Sprinkle
remaining *⅔ cup* onions over
pork. Serve with rice, if desired.

Makes 4 servings

Tip: For a Mediterranean flair,
substitute ½ teaspoon oregano
for ½ teaspoon thyme.

Prep Time: 5 minutes
Cook Time: 15 minutes

Manhattan Turkey à la King

■ ■ ■

8 ounces wide egg noodles
1 pound boneless turkey or
   chicken, cut into strips
1 tablespoon vegetable oil
1 can (14½ ounces) DEL
   MONTE® Pasta Style
   Chunky Tomatoes
1 can (10¾ ounces)
   condensed cream of
   celery soup
1 medium onion, chopped
2 stalks celery, sliced
1 cup sliced mushrooms

1. Cook noodles according to package directions; drain. In large skillet, brown turkey in oil over medium-high heat. Season with salt and pepper, if desired.

2. Add remaining ingredients, except noodles. Cover and cook over medium heat 5 minutes.

3. Remove cover; cook 5 minutes or until thickened, stirring occasionally. Serve over hot noodles. Garnish with chopped parsley, if desired.

Makes 6 servings

Hint: Cook pasta ahead; rinse and drain. Cover and refrigerate. Just before serving, heat in microwave or dip in boiling water.

Prep Time: 7 minutes
Cook Time: 20 minutes

Chicken Carbonara

■ ■ ■

1 pound chicken tenders
1 jar (12 ounces) Alfredo
   sauce
1 cup milk
1⅓ cups FRENCH'S® French
   Fried Onions, divided
½ of a 10-ounce package
   frozen peas, thawed and
   drained
2 tablespoons real bacon
   bits*
   Hot cooked pasta

* Or, substitute 2 strips crumbled, cooked bacon for real bacon bits.

Spray large nonstick skillet with nonstick cooking spray; heat over high heat. Add chicken; cook and stir about 5 minutes or until browned.

Stir in Alfredo sauce and milk. Add ⅔ *cup* French Fried Onions, peas and bacon bits. Bring to a boil. Reduce heat to low. Cook 5 minutes, stirring occasionally. Serve over pasta. Sprinkle with remaining ⅔ *cup* onions.

Makes 4 to 6 servings

Prep Time: 10 minutes
Cook Time: 10 minutes

Eggplant and Feta Skillet

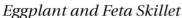

¼ cup olive oil
1 medium eggplant, cut into 1-inch pieces
1 medium zucchini, cut into ½-inch slices
1 package (16 ounces) frozen bell peppers and onions blend, thawed and drained
2 teaspoons bottled minced garlic
2 cans (14½ ounces each) Italian-style diced tomatoes, drained
1 can (2¼ ounces) sliced black olives, drained
1½ cups prepared croutons
¾ cup feta cheese with basil and tomato, crumbled

1. Heat oil in large skillet over high heat until hot.

2. Add eggplant, zucchini, stir-fry blend and garlic; cook and stir 6 minutes. Add tomatoes; simmer 3 minutes. Stir in olives.

3. Sprinkle croutons and feta cheese over top.

Makes 6 servings

Prep and Cook Time:
20 minutes

Eggplant and Feta Skillet

Spicy Mexican Frittata

▌▌▌

1 fresh jalapeño pepper
1 clove garlic
1 medium tomato, peeled, halved, seeded and quartered
½ teaspoon ground coriander
½ teaspoon chili powder
½ cup chopped onion
1 cup frozen corn
6 egg whites
2 eggs
¼ cup skim milk
¼ teaspoon salt
¼ teaspoon black pepper
¼ cup (1 ounce) shredded part-skim farmer or mozzarella cheese

Add jalapeño pepper and garlic to food processor or blender. Process until finely chopped. Add tomato, coriander and chili powder. Cover; process until tomato is almost smooth.

Spray large skillet with nonstick cooking spray; heat skillet over medium heat. Cook and stir onion in hot skillet until tender. Stir in tomato mixture and corn. Cook 3 to 4 minutes or until liquid is almost evaporated, stirring occasionally.

Combine egg whites, eggs, milk, salt and black pepper in medium bowl. Add egg mixture all at once to skillet. Cook, without stirring, 2 minutes or until eggs begin to set. Run large spoon around edge of skillet, lifting eggs for even cooking. Remove skillet from heat when eggs are almost set but surface is still moist.

Sprinkle with cheese. Cover; let stand 3 to 4 minutes or until surface is set and cheese melts. Cut into wedges.

Makes 4 servings

Ham Scramble

▌▌▌

2 tablespoons vegetable oil or butter
1 pound HILLSHIRE FARM® Ham, cut into bite-size pieces
2 onions, thinly sliced
2 apples, cored and sliced

Heat oil in large skillet over medium-high heat. Sauté Ham, onions and apples until onions and apples are tender, stirring constantly.

Makes 4 to 6 servings

Spicy Mexican Frittata

Hearty Hot Dish

▌▌▌

⅓ cup honey
¼ cup spicy brown mustard
¼ cup vegetable oil
1 tablespoon soy sauce
2 cloves garlic, minced
1 teaspoon ground ginger
1 pound HILLSHIRE FARM®
    Beef Smoked Sausage,*
    sliced
2 onions, cut into quarters
1 cup chopped carrots
1 cup chopped celery
1 cup sliced mushrooms

*Or use any variety Hillshire Farm®
Smoked Sausage.*

Combine honey, mustard, oil,
soy sauce, garlic and ginger in
large bowl; blend thoroughly.
Add Smoked Sausage, onions,
carrots, celery and mushrooms.
Saute sausage mixture in large
skillet over medium-high heat
until sausage is lightly
browned.

Makes 4 to 6 servings

Tuna and Rice Skillet Dinner

▌▌▌

1 package (6½ ounces)
    chicken flavored rice mix
½ cup chopped onion
    Water
1½ cups frozen peas and
    carrots, thawed
1 can (10¾ ounces) cream of
    mushroom soup
⅛ teaspoon ground black
    pepper
1 can (12 ounces) STARKIST®
    Solid White or Chunk
    Light Tuna, drained and
    chunked
⅓ cup toasted slivered
    almonds (optional)

In medium saucepan, combine
rice mix and onion; add water.
Prepare rice according to
package directions. Stir in
vegetables, soup and pepper;
blend well. Simmer, covered,
5 to 7 minutes, stirring
occasionally. Stir in tuna; serve
with almonds, if desired.

Makes 4 to 6 servings

Prep Time: 30 minutes

Cook's Notes

When buying new baking
dishes and pans, choose
pieces you can use for
more than one job. For
instance, skillets should
be able to go into
the oven.

Hearty Hot Dish

PIZZA

IN A PINCH

Chicken-Pesto Pizza

▌▌▌

8 ounces chicken tenders
1 medium onion, thinly sliced
⅓ cup prepared pesto
3 medium plum tomatoes,
**   thinly sliced**
1 (14-inch) prepared pizza
**   crust**
1 cup (4 ounces) shredded
**   mozzarella cheese**

1. Preheat oven to 450°F. Cut chicken tenders into bite-size pieces. Coat medium nonstick skillet with nonstick cooking spray; cook and stir chicken over medium heat 2 minutes. Add onion and pesto; cook and stir about 3 minutes or until chicken is cooked through.

2. Arrange tomato slices and chicken mixture on pizza crust to within 1 inch of edge. Sprinkle cheese over topping. Bake 8 minutes or until pizza is hot and cheese is melted and bubbly.   *Makes 6 servings*

Prep and Cook Time:
22 minutes

Niçoise Pizza

▮▮▮

4 ounces goat cheese
½ cup ricotta cheese
½ cup minced fresh basil
1 teaspoon black pepper
1 purchased bread or pizza
 crust (16-ounce size)
2 tablespoons olive oil,
 divided
1 large red onion, sliced
¼ pound fresh young green
 beans, diagonally sliced
1 yellow or red bell pepper,
 cut into thin strips
3 tablespoons sliced black
 olives
½ cup freshly grated
 Parmesan cheese

1. Combine goat cheese, ricotta cheese, basil and black pepper until blended. Spread on bread crust to within ½ inch of edge. Set aside.

2. Preheat oven to 450°F. Heat 1 tablespoon oil in large skillet over medium heat until hot.

3. Add onion to skillet. Cook and stir 8 to 10 minutes or until onion is very tender and brown. Arrange on top of cheese mixture.

4. Heat remaining 1 tablespoon olive oil in same skillet over medium heat until hot. Add beans; cook and stir 1 minute. Add bell pepper; cook and stir

1 minute or until crisp-tender. Arrange on top of onion.

5. Top with olives; sprinkle with Parmesan cheese. Bake 8 to 10 minutes or until bread crust is heated through. Garnish, if desired. *Makes 4 servings*

Pizza Romano

▮▮▮

1 (10-inch) prepared pizza
 crust *or* 4 rounds pita
 bread
1 cup (4 ounces) shredded
 mozzarella cheese
4 slices HILLSHIRE FARM®
 Ham, cut into ½-inch
 strips
1 jar (8 ounces) marinated
 sun-dried tomatoes,
 drained (optional)
1 jar (6 ounces) oil-packed
 artichokes, drained and
 cut into eighths
1 jar (4 ounces) roasted red
 peppers, drained and cut
 into strips

Preheat oven to 425°F.

Place pizza crust on cookie sheet; top with remaining ingredients. Bake on lower rack of oven 15 to 20 minutes or until crust begins to brown lightly and cheese is melted.
 Makes 4 servings

Niçoise Pizza

California Thin Crust Pizza with Smoked Turkey

▎▎▎

1 BUTTERBALL® Fully Cooked Smoked Young Turkey, thawed, sliced thin
½ cup mayonnaise
3 tablespoons grated Parmesan cheese
1 tube (10 ounces) prepared pizza dough
1 teaspoon dried oregano, divided
¼ cup sun-dried tomato bits packed in oil
1 can (14 ounces) artichoke hearts, drained and chopped
1 cup crumbled feta cheese

Combine mayonnaise and Parmesan cheese in small bowl; set aside. Spray 15×10-inch jelly-roll pan with nonstick cooking spray. Press dough into pan. Sprinkle dough with ½ teaspoon oregano. Bake in preheated 425°F oven 8 to 10 minutes or until crust begins to brown. Remove from oven; spread with mayonnaise mixture. Sprinkle turkey, tomato, artichokes and cheese on top of crust. Top with remaining ½ teaspoon oregano. Bake 10 to 12 minutes longer until toppings are heated through.

Makes 24 appetizers

Grilled Vegetables Pizza

▎▎▎

1 teaspoon salt
2 cups (¼-inch) zucchini slices
10 (¼-inch) eggplant slices
2 tablespoons olive oil
1 (12-inch) BOBOLI® Brand Italian Bread Shell
1 cup KRAFT® Shredded Low-Moisture Part-Skim Mozzarella Cheese, divided
¼ cup (¼-inch) roasted red pepper slices
1 tablespoon coarsely chopped fresh basil leaves

Preheat grill. Lightly salt zucchini and eggplant. Brush with oil. Grill on both sides until tender. Sprinkle Boboli® Italian bread shell with ½ cup cheese. Top with grilled vegetables, roasted red peppers, basil and remaining ½ cup cheese. Place bread shell on grill 5 inches from coals. Cover and grill for 3 to 4 minutes or until cheese is melted.

Makes 4 to 6 servings

California Thin Crust Pizza with Smoked Turkey

Pesto Dijon Pizza

▍▍▍

½ cup chopped parsley*
⅓ cup GREY POUPON® Dijon Mustard
¼ cup PLANTERS® Walnuts, chopped*
1 tablespoon olive oil*
2 tablespoons grated Parmesan cheese,* divided
1½ teaspoons dried basil leaves,* divided
2 (8-ounce) packages small prepared pizza crusts
4 ounces thinly sliced deli baked ham
3 plum tomatoes, sliced
1 cup shredded mozzarella cheese (4 ounces)

1 (7-ounce) container prepared pesto sauce may be substituted for parsley, walnuts, olive oil, 1 tablespoon Parmesan cheese and 1 teaspoon basil. Stir mustard into prepared pesto sauce.

In small bowl, combine parsley, mustard, walnuts, oil, 1 tablespoon Parmesan cheese and 1 teaspoon basil. Divide mixture and spread evenly onto each pizza crust. Top each crust with 2 ounces ham, tomato slices and mozzarella cheese. Sprinkle with remaining Parmesan cheese and basil. Place on baking sheet. Bake at 450°F for 8 to 10 minutes or until cheese melts. Cut into wedges; serve warm.

Makes 4 servings

Quattro Formaggio Pizza

▍▍▍

1 (12-inch) Italian bread shell
½ cup prepared pizza or marinara sauce
4 ounces shaved or thinly sliced provolone cheese
1 cup (4 ounces) shredded smoked or regular mozzarella cheese
2 ounces asiago or brick cheese, thinly sliced
¼ cup freshly grated Parmesan or Romano cheese

1. Heat oven to 450°F.

2. Place bread shell on baking sheet. Spread pizza sauce evenly over bread shell.

3. Top sauce with provolone, mozzarella, asiago and Parmesan cheese.

4. Bake 14 minutes or until bread shell is golden brown and cheese is melted.

5. Cut into wedges; serve immediately.

Makes 4 servings

Serving Suggestion: Serve with a tossed green salad.

Prep and Cook Time: 26 minutes

Pesto Dijon Pizza

Pizza with Fontina, Artichoke Hearts and Red Onion

■ ■ ■

1 pound frozen white bread dough, thawed according to package directions
2 tablespoons olive oil, divided
2 tablespoons wheat bran
1 large clove garlic, minced
½ red onion, thinly sliced
1 package (9 ounces) frozen artichoke hearts, thawed and sliced lengthwise
Salt and black pepper
1 cup (4 ounces) shredded Wisconsin Fontina cheese

Preheat oven to 450°F. On lightly oiled baking sheet, press chilled dough into 12×9-inch rectangle; crimp edges to form rim. Brush with 1 tablespoon oil. Evenly sprinkle with bran; press lightly into dough. Sprinkle with garlic. Arrange onion in 1 layer over dough; top with artichoke hearts. Drizzle with remaining 1 tablespoon oil. Lightly season with salt and pepper. Evenly sprinkle with cheese. (Do not let dough rise.) Bake 15 minutes or until crust is golden brown.

Makes 4 servings

Favorite recipe from **Wisconsin Milk Marketing Board**

Barbecue Pizza

■ ■ ■

2 teaspoons olive oil
1 boneless skinless chicken breast (about 5 ounces), cut into ¾-inch cubes
3 ounces HILLSHIRE FARM® Pepperoni, sliced
⅓ cup barbecue sauce, divided
1 (12-inch) prepared pizza crust
1¼ cups shredded mozzarella cheese, divided
2 tablespoons thinly sliced green onion tops

Preheat oven to 450°F.

Heat oil in small skillet over medium-high heat. Sauté chicken until barely done, 3 to 5 minutes. Remove from heat and pour off juices. Add Pepperoni and 1 tablespoon barbecue sauce to chicken. Stir to mix and separate slices.

Spread remaining barbecue sauce over pizza crust. Sprinkle ¾ cup cheese over sauce. Sprinkle pepperoni mixture over cheese; sprinkle with green onion. Top with remaining ½ cup cheese. Place in oven directly on oven rack. Bake 8 to 10 minutes or until cheese is bubbly and pizza crust is crisp.

Makes 4 to 6 servings

Barbecue Pizza

Thai Chicken Pizza

███

2 boneless skinless chicken
    breast halves (½ pound)
2 teaspoons Thai seasoning
    Nonstick cooking spray
2 tablespoons pineapple juice
1 tablespoon peanut butter
1 tablespoon oyster sauce
1 teaspoon Thai chili paste*
2 (10-inch) flour tortillas
½ cup shredded carrot
½ cup sliced green onions
½ cup red bell pepper slices
¼ cup chopped cilantro
½ cup (2 ounces) shredded
    part-skim mozzarella
    cheese

Thai chili paste is available at some larger supermarkets and at Oriental markets.

1. Preheat oven to 400°F. Cut chicken breasts crosswise into thin slices, each about 1½×½ inch. Sprinkle with Thai seasoning. Let stand 5 minutes. Spray large nonstick skillet with cooking spray; heat over medium heat until hot. Add chicken. Cook and stir 3 minutes or until chicken is lightly browned and no longer pink in center.

2. Combine pineapple juice, peanut butter, oyster sauce and chili paste in small bowl until smooth. Place tortillas on baking sheets. Spread peanut butter mixture over tortillas. Divide chicken, carrot, green onions, pepper and cilantro evenly between each tortilla. Sprinkle with cheese. Bake 5 minutes or until tortillas are crisp and cheese is melted. Cut into wedges.

Makes 4 servings

Cook's Notes

Oyster sauce is a thick, brown, concentrated sauce made of ground oysters, soy sauce and brine. It imparts very little fish flavor to foods and is used as a seasoning to intensify other flavors.

Thai Chicken Pizza

SANDWICH
EXPRESS

Monte Cristo Sandwiches

⅓ cup **HELLMANN'S®** or **BEST FOODS®** Real or Light Mayonnaise or Low Fat Mayonnaise Dressing
¼ teaspoon ground nutmeg
⅛ teaspoon freshly ground pepper
12 slices white bread, crusts removed
6 slices Swiss cheese
6 slices cooked ham
6 slices cooked chicken
2 eggs
½ cup milk

1. In small bowl, combine mayonnaise, nutmeg and pepper; spread on one side of each bread slice.

2. Layer cheese, ham and chicken on 6 bread slices; top with remaining bread, mayonnaise sides down. Cut sandwiches diagonally into quarters.

3. In small bowl, beat together eggs and milk; dip sandwich quarters into egg mixture.

4. Cook on preheated greased griddle or in skillet, turning once, 4 to 5 minutes or until browned and heated through.
Makes 24 mini sandwiches

Eggplant & Pepper Cheese Sandwiches

1 (8-ounce) eggplant, cut into 18 slices
Salt and black pepper, to taste
⅓ cup GREY POUPON® COUNTRY DIJON® Mustard
¼ cup olive oil
2 tablespoons red wine vinegar
¾ teaspoon dried oregano leaves
1 clove garlic, crushed
6 (4-inch) pieces French bread, cut in half
1 (7-ounce) jar roasted red peppers, cut into strips
1½ cups shredded mozzarella cheese (6 ounces)

Place eggplant slices on greased baking sheet, overlapping slightly. Sprinkle lightly with salt and pepper. Bake at 400°F for 10 to 12 minutes or until tender.

Blend mustard, oil, vinegar, oregano and garlic. Brush eggplant slices with ¼ cup mustard mixture; broil eggplant for 1 minute.

Brush cut sides of French bread with remaining mustard mixture. Layer 3 slices eggplant, a few red pepper strips and ¼ cup cheese on each bread bottom. Place on broiler pan with roll tops, cut-sides up; broil until cheese melts. Close sandwiches with bread tops and serve immediately; garnish as desired.

Makes 6 sandwiches

Cook's Nook

When purchasing eggplant, look for a firm eggplant that is heavy for its size, with a tight glossy, deeply-colored skin. The stem should be bright green. Dull skin and rust-colored spots are a sign of old age. Refrigerate unwashed eggplant in a plastic bag for up to 5 days.

Eggplant & Pepper Cheese Sandwiches

Bistro Turkey Sandwiches

■ ■ ■

¼ cup reduced-calorie
    mayonnaise
2 tablespoons finely chopped
    fresh basil
2 tablespoons chopped
    drained sun-dried
    tomatoes in oil
2 tablespoons finely chopped
    pitted kalamata olives
⅛ teaspoon red pepper flakes
1 loaf focaccia bread,
    quartered and split *or*
    8 slices sourdough bread
1 jar (7 ounces) roasted red
    bell peppers, rinsed and
    drained
4 romaine or red leaf lettuce
    leaves
2 packages (4 ounces each)
    HEBREW NATIONAL®
    Sliced Oven Roasted or
    Smoked Turkey Breast

Combine mayonnaise, basil,
sun-dried tomatoes, olives and
red pepper in small bowl; mix
well. Spread evenly over cut
sides of bread. Remove excess
liquid from roasted red bell
peppers with paper towels.
Layer roasted peppers, lettuce
and turkey breast between
bread slices.

Makes 4 servings

Amigo Pita Pocket Sandwiches

■ ■ ■

1 pound ground turkey
1 can (7 ounces) whole
    kernel corn, drained
1 can (6 ounces) tomato
    paste
½ cup water
½ cup chopped green bell
    pepper
1 package (1.0 ounce)
    LAWRY'S® Taco Spices &
    Seasonings
8 pita breads
    Curly lettuce leaves
    Shredded Cheddar cheese

In large skillet, brown ground
turkey until no longer pink;
drain fat. Add corn, tomato
paste, water, bell pepper and
Taco Spices & Seasonings; mix
well. Bring to a boil over
medium-high heat; reduce heat
to low and cook, uncovered, 15
minutes. Cut off top quarter of
pita breads and open to form
pockets. Line each with lettuce
leaves. Spoon about ½ cup
filling into each pita bread and
top with cheese.

Makes 8 servings

Serving Suggestion: Serve with
vegetable sticks and fresh fruit.

Bistro Turkey Sandwich

French Dip Sandwiches

½ cup A.1.® Original or A.1.® Bold & Spicy Steak Sauce, divided
1 tablespoon GREY POUPON® Dijon Mustard
4 steak rolls, split horizontally
8 ounces sliced cooked roast beef
1 (13¾-fluid ounce) can beef broth

In small bowl, blend ¼ cup steak sauce and mustard; spread mixture evenly on cut sides of roll tops. Arrange 2 ounces beef on each roll bottom; replace roll tops over beef. Slice sandwiches in half crosswise if desired. In small saucepan, heat broth and remaining ¼ cup steak sauce, stirring occasionally. Serve as a dipping sauce with sandwiches. Garnish as desired.

Makes 4 servings

French Dip Sandwich

Grilled Eggplant Sandwiches

▌▌▌

1 eggplant (about 1¼ pounds)
Salt and black pepper
6 thin slices provolone cheese
6 thin slices deli-style ham or mortadella
Fresh basil leaves (optional)
Olive oil

Cut eggplant into 12 (⅜-inch-thick) rounds; sprinkle both sides with salt and pepper. Top each of 6 eggplant slices with slice of cheese, slice of meat (fold or tear to fit) and a few basil leaves, if desired. Cover with slice of eggplant. Brush one side with olive oil. Secure each sandwich with 2 or 3 toothpicks.

Oil hot grid to help prevent sticking. Grill eggplant, oil side down, on covered grill, over medium **KINGSFORD®** briquets, 15 to 20 minutes. Halfway through cooking time, brush top with oil, then turn and continue grilling until eggplant is tender when pierced. (When turning, position sandwiches so toothpicks extend down between spaces in grid.) If eggplant starts to char, move to cooler part of grill.

Let sandwiches cool about 5 minutes, then cut into halves or quarters, if desired. Serve warm or at room temperature.

Makes 6 sandwiches

Mediterranean Pita Sandwiches

▌▌▌

1 cup plain nonfat yogurt
1 tablespoon chopped fresh cilantro
2 cloves garlic, minced
1 teaspoon lemon juice
1 can (15 ounces) chick-peas, drained and rinsed
1 can (14 ounces) cooked artichoke hearts, drained, rinsed and coarsely chopped
1½ cups thinly sliced cucumbers, cut into halves
½ cup shredded carrot
½ cup chopped green onions
4 whole wheat pitas, cut into halves

1. Combine yogurt, cilantro, garlic and lemon juice in small bowl.

2. Combine chick-peas, artichoke hearts, cucumbers, carrot and green onions in medium bowl. Stir in yogurt mixture until well blended. Divide cucumber mixture among pita halves.

Makes 4 servings

Mediterranean Chicken Salad Sandwiches

▌▌▌

4 boneless skinless chicken breast halves
1 teaspoon dried basil leaves
¼ teaspoon salt
¼ teaspoon black pepper
1 cup chopped cucumber
½ cup mayonnaise
¼ cup chopped roasted red pepper
¼ cup pitted black olive slices
¼ cup yogurt
¼ teaspoon garlic powder
6 Kaiser rolls, split
   Additional mayonnaise
   Lettuce leaves

Place chicken, ½ cup water, basil, salt and pepper in medium saucepan; bring to a boil. Reduce heat; simmer covered 10 to 12 minutes or until chicken is no longer pink in center. Remove chicken from saucepan; cool. Cut into ½-inch pieces.

Combine chicken, cucumber, mayonnaise, red pepper, olives, yogurt and garlic powder in medium bowl; toss to coat well.

Spread rolls with additional mayonnaise. Top with lettuce and chicken salad mixture.
Makes 6 servings

Philadelphia Cheese Steak Sandwiches

▌▌▌

2 cups sliced red or green bell peppers (about 2 medium)
1 small onion, thinly sliced
1 tablespoon vegetable oil
½ cup A.1.® Original or A.1.® Bold & Spicy Steak Sauce
1 teaspoon prepared horseradish
8 ounces thinly sliced beef sandwich steaks
4 ounces thinly sliced mozzarella cheese
4 long sandwich rolls, split

In medium saucepan, over medium heat, sauté pepper and onion slices in oil until tender. Stir in steak sauce and horseradish; keep warm.

In lightly greased medium skillet, over medium-high heat, cook sandwich steaks until done. Portion beef, pepper mixture and cheese on roll bottoms.

Broil sandwich bottoms 4 inches from heat source for 3 to 5 minutes or until cheese melts; replace tops. Serve immediately.
Makes 4 sandwiches

Philadelphia Cheese Steak Sandwich

Spicy Sesame Turkey Sandwich

½ cup mayonnaise
1½ teaspoons LAWRY'S® Pinch of Herbs, divided
1½ teaspoons LAWRY'S® Lemon Pepper, divided
1 teaspoon sesame oil
1 teaspoon fresh lemon juice
4 or 5 turkey cutlets (about 1¼ pounds)
½ cup all-purpose flour
2 tablespoons toasted sesame seeds
¼ to ½ teaspoon cayenne pepper
¼ cup milk
¼ cup vegetable oil
6 whole wheat buns, toasted
1 tomato, cut into 6 slices
6 sprigs watercress

In small bowl, combine mayonnaise, ½ teaspoon Pinch of Herbs, ½ teaspoon Lemon Pepper, sesame oil and lemon juice; cover. Refrigerate until ready to serve. Cut turkey into six equal portions. In large resealable plastic food storage bag, combine flour, sesame seeds, cayenne pepper, remaining Pinch of Herbs and remaining Lemon Pepper. Dip each turkey cutlet into milk. Add turkey, a few pieces at a time, to plastic bag; seal bag. Shake until well coated. In large, heavy skillet, heat oil. Add turkey; cook over medium heat 5 to 8 minutes or until no longer pink in center, turning halfway through cooking time. Spread cut sides of buns with mayonnaise mixture. Top bottom half of each bun with turkey; cover with tomato, watercress and top half of roll.

Makes 6 servings

Serving Suggestion: Serve with coleslaw and juicy watermelon.

Cook's Notes

To toast sesame seeds, spread the seeds out in a small skillet. Shake the skillet over medium heat for 2 minutes or until the seeds begin to pop and turn golden.

DOUBLE-TIME

Grasshopper Pie

- **2 cups graham cracker crumbs**
- **4 tablespoons unsweetened cocoa powder**
- **¼ cup margarine, melted**
- **8 ounces nonfat cream cheese, softened**
- **1 cup low-fat (1%) milk**
- **2 tablespoons green crème de menthe liqueur**
- **2 tablespoons white crème de menthe liqueur**
- **1½ teaspoons vanilla**
- **1 container (4 ounces) frozen whipped topping, thawed**

Spray 9-inch pie plate with nonstick cooking spray. Combine cracker crumbs, cocoa and margarine in medium bowl. Press onto bottom and up side of prepared pie plate. Refrigerate. Beat cream cheese in large bowl with electric mixer until fluffy. Gradually beat in milk until smooth. Stir in both liqueurs and vanilla. Fold in whipped topping. Refrigerate 20 minutes or until chilled, but not set. Pour into chilled crust. Freeze 4 hours or until set.

Makes 8 servings

DESSERTS

Oreo® Cheesecake

■ ■ ■

1 (20-ounce) package OREO®
    Chocolate Sandwich
    Cookies
⅓ cup margarine, melted
3 (8-ounce) packages cream
    cheese, softened
¾ cup sugar
4 eggs, at room temperature
1 cup dairy sour cream
1 teaspoon vanilla
    Whipped cream for garnish

Preheat oven to 350°F. Finely
roll 30 cookies; coarsely chop
20 cookies. In medium bowl,
combine finely rolled cookie
crumbs and margarine. Press
on bottom and 2 inches up side
of 9-inch springform pan; set
aside.

In large bowl with electric
mixer at medium speed, beat
cream cheese and sugar until
creamy. Blend in eggs, sour
cream and vanilla; fold in
chopped cookies. Spread
mixture into prepared crust.
Bake at 350°F 60 minutes or
until set.

Cool on wire rack at room
temperature. Chill at least 4
hours. Halve remaining
cookies; remove side of pan. To
serve, garnish with whipped
cream and cookie halves.

Makes 12 servings

Mocha Parfaits

■ ■ ■

1½ tablespoons margarine
⅓ cup unsweetened cocoa
    powder
1 cup boiling water
½ cup sugar
1 tablespoon instant coffee
    granules
1 teaspoon vanilla
1 pint coffee-flavored nonfat
    frozen yogurt
12 whole coffee beans
    (optional)

1. Melt margarine in heavy
saucepan over low heat. Add
cocoa; cook and stir 3 minutes.
Add boiling water, sugar and
coffee; cook and stir until
thickened. Remove from heat;
stir in vanilla. Cool.

2. Place 2 tablespoons frozen
yogurt in bottom of each of 4
parfait glasses. Top each with 1
tablespoon sauce. Top sauce
with another 2 tablespoons
frozen yogurt; top frozen yogurt
with 2 tablespoons sauce.
Repeat layering twice more. Top
each parfait with 3 coffee
beans, if desired.

Makes 4 servings

Mocha Parfaits

Sundae Shortcakes

▐▐▐

1 cup sugar
⅓ cup thawed frozen orange juice concentrate
3 tablespoons butter or margarine
1 can (17.3 ounces) refrigerated buttermilk biscuits
1 pint frozen vanilla or fruit-flavored yogurt or vanilla ice cream
3 cups fresh or frozen blackberries, thawed
Frozen whipped topping

1. Combine sugar, orange juice concentrate, ⅓ cup water and butter in small saucepan. Bring to a boil over medium-high heat, stirring constantly until sugar is melted. Boil gently, uncovered, 5 minutes.

2. Prepare biscuits according to package directions. Pierce 4 biscuits all over with skewer. Spoon ¼ of sugar mixture over 4 biscuits. Reserve remaining biscuits for another use. Let stand 1 minute.

3. Split biscuits; place bottom halves on serving plates. Spoon yogurt evenly over bottoms; top with blackberries. Drizzle with remaining sugar mixture; top with biscuit tops.

Makes 4 servings

Serving Suggestion: Serve with frozen whipped topping.

Prep and Cook Time: 30 minutes

Magic Dip

▐▐▐

1 package (8 ounces) PHILADELPHIA BRAND® Cream Cheese, softened
1 cup BAKER'S® Semi-Sweet Real Chocolate Chips
½ cup BAKER'S® ANGEL FLAKE® Coconut, toasted
½ cup chopped peanuts

SPREAD cream cheese on bottom of 9-inch microwavable pie plate or quiche dish.

TOP with remaining ingredients.

MICROWAVE on MEDIUM (50% power) 3 to 4 minutes or until warm. Serve with graham crackers. Garnish, if desired.

Makes 6 to 8 servings

Prep Time: 5 minutes
Microwave Time: 4 minutes

Magic Dip

Cherry Cheesecake Squares

▮▮▮

2 cups graham cracker
crumbs
¼ cup sugar
¼ cup (½ stick) butter or
margarine, melted
3 packages (8 ounces each)
PHILADELPHIA BRAND®
Cream Cheese, softened
¾ cup sugar
1 teaspoon vanilla
2 eggs
1 can (20 ounces) cherry pie
filling

MIX crumbs, ¼ cup sugar and butter. Press into 13×9-inch baking pan. Bake at 325°F for 10 minutes.

MIX cream cheese, ¾ cup sugar and vanilla with electric mixer on medium speed until well blended. Add eggs; mix just until blended. Pour over crust.

BAKE at 325°F for 35 minutes or until center is almost set. Cool. Refrigerate 3 hours or overnight. Top with pie filling. Cut into squares.

Makes 18 servings

Prep Time: 20 minutes plus refrigerating
Bake Time: 35 minutes

Caramelized Peaches & Cream

▮▮▮

2 pounds sliced peeled
unsweetened peaches or
thawed and well-drained
frozen peaches
2 tablespoons bourbon
¾ cup reduced-fat sour cream
½ teaspoon ground cinnamon
¼ teaspoon ground nutmeg
¾ cup packed light brown
sugar
8 slices (1½ ounces each)
angel food cake

1. Toss peaches with bourbon in shallow ovenproof 1½-quart casserole or 11×7-inch glass baking dish. Press down into even layer.

2. Combine sour cream, cinnamon and nutmeg in small bowl; mix well. Spoon mixture evenly over peaches. (May be covered and refrigerated up to 2 hours before cooking time.)

3. Preheat broiler. Sprinkle brown sugar evenly over sour cream mixture to cover. Broil 4 to 5 inches from heat, 3 to 5 minutes or until brown sugar is melted and bubbly. (Watch closely after 3 minutes so that sugar does not burn.)

4. Spoon immediately over angel food cake.

Makes 8 servings

Blueberry Dream Fritters

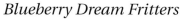

Vegetable oil
½ cup whipping cream
1 egg
1 teaspoon vanilla
1 cup self-rising flour
⅓ cup self-rising cornmeal
⅓ cup sugar
1½ cups fresh blueberries

1. Heat 2 inches oil in large heavy skillet to 375°F on deep-fat thermometer.

2. Meanwhile, stir together cream, egg and vanilla.

3. Combine flour, cornmeal and sugar in large bowl. Stir in cream mixture just until moistened. Fold in blueberries.

4. Carefully drop batter by heaping tablespoonfuls into hot oil. Fry until golden brown, turning once. Drain well on paper towels.

Makes 12 fritters

Serving Suggestion: Sprinkle fritters with powdered sugar.

Prep and Cook Time: 19 minutes

Blueberry Dream Fritters

Strawberry Margarita Pie

▌▌▌

3 tablespoons margarine
2 tablespoons honey
1½ cups crushed pretzels
3 cups low-fat sugar-free
    strawberry frozen yogurt,
    softened
1½ cups light nondairy whipped
    topping, thawed
2 teaspoons grated lime peel,
    divided
1 package (16 ounces)
    strawberries in syrup,
    thawed
1 tablespoon lime juice
1 tablespoon tequila
    (optional)

1. Combine margarine and honey in medium microwavable bowl. Microwave on HIGH 30 seconds or until smooth when stirred. Add pretzels; stir until evenly coated. Press into bottom and side of 9-inch pie plate; freeze 30 minutes or until firm.

2. Combine frozen yogurt, whipped topping and 1 teaspoon lime peel in medium bowl; gently fold with rubber spatula or wire whisk. Spoon into pie plate. Freeze 2 hours or until firm.

3. Combine strawberries, lime juice and remaining 1 teaspoon peel in small bowl; stir to blend.

4. Cut pie into 8 portions; serve with strawberry mixture. Add tequila to strawberry mixture just before serving, if desired.

Makes 8 servings

Mango Coconut Tropical Freeze

▌▌▌

1 jar (26 ounces) refrigerated
    mango slices, drained (or
    the flesh of 3 ripe
    mangoes, peeled and cut
    to equal about 3⅓ cups)
½ cup canned coconut cream
1 tablespoon lime juice
⅓ cup toasted chopped
    pecans

1. Place mango, coconut cream and lime juice in food processor; process 1 to 2 minutes or until smooth.

2. Spoon into small dessert cups or custard cups. Top with pecans. Place cups on pie plate, cover tightly. Freeze 8 hours or overnight. Remove from freezer and allow to thaw slightly before serving. Serve immediately.

Makes 4 servings

Make-Ahead Time: up to 1 day before serving
Final Prep Time: about 30 minutes

Strawberry Margarita Pie

ACKNOWLEDGMENTS

The publishers would like to thank the companies and organizations listed below for the use of their recipes and photographs in this publication.

A.1.® Steak Sauce

Bestfoods

Birds Eye®

Butterball® Turkey Company

Del Monte Corporation

Egg Beaters® Healthy Real Egg Substitute

GREY POUPON® Mustard

Hebrew National®

Hillshire Farm®

The HV Company

Kikkoman International Inc.

The Kingsford Products Company

Kraft Foods, Inc.

Lawry's® Foods, Inc.

Lipton®

OREO® Cookies

The Procter & Gamble Company

Reckitt & Colman Inc.

The J.M. Smucker Company

StarKist® Seafood Company

Veg-All®

Wisconsin Milk Marketing Board

INDEX

METRIC CONVERSION CHART

VOLUME MEASUREMENTS (dry)

⅛ teaspoon = 0.5 mL

¼ teaspoon = 1 mL

½ teaspoon = 2 mL

¾ teaspoon = 4 mL

1 teaspoon = 5 mL

1 tablespoon = 15 mL

2 tablespoons = 30 mL

¼ cup = 60 mL

⅓ cup = 75 mL

½ cup = 125 mL

⅔ cup = 150 mL

¾ cup = 175 mL

1 cup = 250 mL

2 cups = 1 pint = 500 mL

3 cups = 750 mL

4 cups = 1 quart = 1 L

VOLUME MEASUREMENTS (fluid)

1 fluid ounce (2 tablespoons) = 30 mL

4 fluid ounces (½ cup) = 125 mL

8 fluid ounces (1 cup) = 250 mL

12 fluid ounces (1½ cups) = 375 mL

16 fluid ounces (2 cups) = 500 mL

WEIGHTS (mass)

½ ounce = 15 g

1 ounce = 30 g

3 ounces = 90 g

4 ounces = 120 g

8 ounces = 225 g

10 ounces = 285 g

12 ounces = 360 g

16 ounces = 1 pound = 450 g

DIMENSIONS

1/16 inch = 2 mm

⅛ inch = 3 mm

¼ inch = 6 mm

½ inch = 1.5 cm

¾ inch = 2 cm

1 inch = 2.5 cm

OVEN TEMPERATURES

250°F = 120°C

275°F = 140°C

300°F = 150°C

325°F = 160°C

350°F = 180°C

375°F = 190°C

400°F = 200°C

425°F = 220°C

450°F = 230°C

BAKING PAN SIZES

Utensil	Size in Inches/Quarts	Metric Volume	Size in Centimeters
Baking or Cake Pan (square or rectangular)	8×8×2	2 L	20×20×5
	9×9×2	2.5 L	23×23×5
	12×8×2	3 L	30×20×5
	13×9×2	3.5 L	33×23×5
Loaf Pan	8×4×3	1.5 L	20×10×7
	9×5×3	2 L	23×13×7
Round Layer Cake Pan	8×1½	1.2 L	20×4
	9×1½	1.5 L	23×4
Pie Plate	8×1¼	750 mL	20×3
	9×1¼	1 L	23×3
Baking Dish or Casserole	1 quart	1 L	—
	1½ quart	1.5 L	—
	2 quart	2 L	—